The waiting

winner of the IOWA POETRY PRIZE

MEGAN JOHNSON

The waiting

UNIVERSITY OF IOWA PRESS Ψ IOWA CITY

University of Iowa Press, Iowa City 52242

Printed in the United States of America
Design by Richard Hendel
http://www.uiowa.edu/uiowapress

The University of Iowa Press is a member of
Green Press Initiative and is committed to preserving
natural resources.

Printed on acid-free paper

Library of Congress Cataloging-in-Publication Data
Johnson, Megan, 1976–.
The waiting / by Megan Johnson.
p.   cm. — (The Iowa poetry prize)
ISBN 0-87745-924-X (pbk.)
I. Title.   II. Series.
PS3610.O366W35 2005
811'.6 — dc22   2004059828
05 06 07 08 09 P 5 4 3 2 1

For my family

and

For Reginald

Contents

Acknowledgments

Grateful acknowledgments to the following journals in which some of these poems, sometimes in a different form, first appeared:

Interim, "I am inside this flag"; *Colorado Review*, "Wing for unaware"; *Verse*, "Still life with weave"; *Turbine*, "Nocturne 1," "Nocturne 2," and "Nocturne 3"; and the *Antioch Review*, "Through my chest, where were you."

All italicized text in "Getting ready for time" is taken from William Faulkner's *As I Lay Dying*.

Many thanks to Don Revell, Claudia Keelan, Reginald Shepherd, Carrie Bennett, Lilly Roberts, Ian Stansel, Jen Blair, my fantastic parents, and the various manifestations of the Java House poetry group for their encouragement and readership. Special thanks to Scott Christian Hage, whose unfaltering support keeps me alive and well.

For his generous financial support, thank you, Glenn Schaeffer.

A million thanks to Rachel Beck, whose careful eye and ear has helped in making these poems what they are.

And to Mark Levine: my unending gratitude.

I

How it comes to pass

See here   little faltering one
          that radio song is for you   a top ten hit
ten years ago   and the car   gently nudges
          the house   where air circulation
is bad   you can't breathe   correctly
          not getting the sap   under your nails
is a shame   this earth can bear   almonds
          can't you stand a little straighter
even though the limelight   not meant for you
          looks luscious on skin   whose is it
two bodies converging   when does it happen
          when the taste of salt   sticks for days
you grow old   the kite at its peak
          can drift for hours   if the wind is right —

Tradition, only the present

Hazy to meet here, pacing,
deciphering sky speech,
factors sweeping willows to dirt &
bound to what the tongue cannot see.
I make my bed. I sleep on the floor.
I was sitting onward and upward,
feeling my way between piano chords,
the way not attached to the escalator,
Mars hanging in the atmosphere
like a ghost town rearranged.
What carrot, now, will I give to the goat
whose crocheted eyes are only needy?
Who will remember the cracked stein in the heap?
The blushing disembodied cannot hear
the bike chains clinking poles,
reverberate, defenestrate, last words in
drifting balloon high above our heads. But
serious & dark & wind pitching tents within
the saved pebbles in my pocket.
But lukewarm & sliding, standing there before
the termites reach my hands.

Still life with weave

Bruised the day myself, no rotten fruit parallel or adjacent.
Outside, those meticulous woods named *hold still* flapping and flapping —

Forget the planted seeds, mistress of the mister latching quietly the back door.
Honey drip slow are you going is the bottle overrun by forgetfulness.

Last time on vacation the postcard didn't compare
to weather shaking boughs of bridges: wood creak: performance.

Smeared the window but I wanted you exact. Bodily whisk
me to a feather bed, the air moisture soft and a large drink to taste.

Stillness subjected to a motorcycle vavooming its way to Maine,
suitcase waterproofed and city decals faded attest

and keep bustling we will get there the gas tank half full.
My profile as much a place as any, *San Miguel, San Marino* faceless.

One horse in the woods not moving to apologize for the trickle,
small stream washed you naked me elsewhere the wine just so the tablecloth just so

let mister in it's a feast today, frequent the small talk unfolding there is honey
enough to make do, musicians booked from out of town: chamber music: solo

driver it is not a racetrack *allegro to halt* so many delicious undertakings
I shake then stop the window shatter you can smell the peaches pears

the bed's backbone is awash and cannot reach ground.

Seasons (trying to align)

Down in front, the way across
        the field, some orchids, mums, hatbox discarded.
   No use,
      sandblasted & minuscule stumbling.
Sun descending on first yellow leaf glares,
      camera failing us again
        and why not leave flotation devices for another day —
      (Marry me quick sir get-it-together. Once I stood, head of hail,
wordless and smack dab in the middle. Once I flew a kite into cold rain
      the story gained a new undertaker —)
Conversation drowned in construction, nearby, dirt, rain, mud, sun, dirt;
      smooth road, shovels on a truck-out-of-town
        faster than a wishbone snap.
A betrayal and a slim squirrel hoarding for winter —
      Just as the willows perk up, my darkening face.
       (Back-in-a-flash I name you, aching head, and yes,
        I consumed my stars)
Tending sight I let the rabid dog have a run of it,
      a recourse, a beehive less swarm and sting
       trampled in sea —
    (My oh my we're cliff-ridden, maps not jotted
       yet I'm standing)
Warp of gesture, debris coalescing —
      Sparrow song through a summer wine bag: I do.
      Saunter home to the red hot —

Circumference

Limelight: the steady field dissipates.
Every fall leaves rain in a storm of disbelief.

How the self-contained tree casts
them out of altitude in fistfuls.

I worked the 9 to 5 gravitational pull.
Placed my compass under the hatchet and

hauled my boundaries into the closet.
Stowaway show, opera of leaves dismantled.

Meaty thoughts loop and you on another
continent where it is obliquely raining.

This angle I am among the captured field, can
root the flowers' grip, outline the leaves in dusty chalk.

An airplane treads on the lungs of a loose cloud.
I read beneath the closet from no light

and each letter forms the shape
of an icy sled rounding the curve.

I only divided you with the words
oyster and *slicker* and *come home*.

The sun bites down on day or prepares to fall.

Rocket grass

Becomes a way of saying
            the back of my neck tightened to a T
     and forgiving you is a boathouse off the shore and
                cannot while away each ant in the aching sun
     (a song I like to hold my hands still nervous fingers)
              (the cut of grass early and full of diamonds)
I mean all these things
                a caboose whittled down to stone
                   the children's pool dusted with urine
          vain hush from a voice in the back row
                     (hungry picnic at our feet almost forgotten)
   The small bundles with stork feathers still attached
            arriving when tossed and turned you're too hot
               you're too cold a night-light eliminating uncertainties
       this backbone which is home and bed and the grass
                    they'll bury me under —
Show me again the limp cotton drying
         wet world inside a paperweight
               hybrid rock and sickle cell whose morse
             embedded in my palm
          can hear me breathe you breathing back a body
    (not concocted response) and wine shines like
memory sandbagged   discerning flowers from weeds
        brightly calling and on the moon I too walked softly —
I have rearranged your eyes into glass pinecones
        and the murmuring logic and the hay stack sculptures
            disintegrating a little more each day with wind —

A little / more

Summer proximity you should
have known me.
        These stretched arms supposed —
            The candle burning —
                I, the days worth missing.

*

Underneath the lamp
        a fiery sheen   could you
              gain up to.
And this sick certainty I do not
        want to give you, most days
I plant ferns.   A little hatching
       into.

*

Single egg of one yolk,
        you happen this way.
           I do not want to   focus on the split.
Hubris or shame
        it is the end of the day; there are
          common denominators.

*

At this moment the
                first stop sign dismantled.
Lately, fine. I said box the matter
                                I said sing the scream.
The wool not as coarse as you thought —

*

I meant weather miracle
                till the sky.
                                See the way
                my hands mean?
It was a courageous act: a boy   some fire
                voice.   You could always
option down the next block.

*

Clearly the simultaneity held my hand —
                this house   my lesser instance —
        Sun dim,   a horrific.
Free the blinds, please, only don't.
                You exhausted into day.
                                (I am more than a little.)

*

So much garbage in the garbage
                can you let it?
Boundary me silent   reinvest the gesture.
                Sometimes doesn't it,
        not quite an explosion,
                                ungraceful hand.
        I am calling you out of —

Enter an empty flowerpot

Wet dirt clots
its mineral supply.
      Harvest the salty rain,
      flourish from here
      to the fullest metronoming cloud.
Drops litter the entrance
I braked with blocks.
      Once the city gave its lamps
      a statue to shine for and
      once I trailed behind
      a season skipping
      hot pebbles through
      a frozen pond.
I fast forward
when I don't like the song.
      Taxicab thrifting our fare
      to neighborhoods
      that vowel like ours.
Fertilizer proved a makeshift
failure and the red wine
blemish won't come out.
      I clear salt grains from
      the cold dinner table.
During death the iris
browns till its limbs
recede from the body.
      The occasion takes
      weeks to fulfill.

Stage left an umbrella

Dark the audience pinned to gravel and crunch.
       Look, the relative mountain
       has litters of local names.
I parade by for a drink.
       Claustrophobia was possible
       save your hands
       outlined by moon.
Early on fruit plunged into bags.
Early on hid in the light
       to thick miles
       repeating *dirt*.
My car's engine fell out.
       Plastic chairs fused
       our sturdy study.
Copper cornfield in my pocket.
       No heaving water planned
       to outluck your stars.
And when the bough breaks.
And when the bough breaks.
       Storm comes. Flash.

II

Why not matter

The details of trees summer me slow. Green and then shadow, he and I brisk at the party at the capitulation of drinks I have forgotten their names — the new sofa is new only to me, all the minutes riding a steep horse. I want to go home away from each branch entwined with its neighbor. Such delicious eyesores the bare toes are, when will he stop driving that car into that lake and dance. Could I say stars, stripes, how the moon's holed up in daylight? Stick in a dog's mouth. He calls my name by thick degrees and sweat. Please open the city so I can laugh openly with sparrow-slick flight. Newspaper clippings, a little red plastic cup; please witness and rebook the water is turning lukewarm. Today the sky contains the usual sky-things. He is afraid his haircut isn't matching. Burrs in my pocket. Would he extract some limestone from that riverbed.

Why not bombard, all this heat

Lucky to taste strawberries. In June begging is a bell circling the pretty park people, not quite dusk. Get on with it I keep saying, presentation must be the luckiest form we serve on a lust platter. Market thick, can't see past that woman's scarf. Halfway orange, pink, or perhaps the tight watermelons have just come into view. Junk in the sale, but shiny junk. Near the edge two dogs with two leashes; I count out the dollar in my pocket. Haze too redundant to get a good look at. Groves all the way from one snippet. Toss of the hair, popsicle teeth. What a barnyard affair across the flags at full height. I like the way you shift, how I look in the mirror and see nothing.

Why not trivialize, surely we love the alphabet

Here the curtains blow so the wind is actual, I am trying to get a fistful. Let's repeat the looks on those lovers' faces and fail. The glass keeps most of the water, downstairs fruit rots, remember the time you lost the race with the clouds it was only last Sunday — During the hit and run I have little to say. Only, your hand with its broken thumb and I'm fat as a house. And bust up the silence only don't use my prize rocks. Golden raincoat in the closet extinguishing. Watering the seeds a daily event, fresh tips, porch sagging with rain. Yes, that grocery store certainly does have the freshest broccoli in town. Salty margarita glass. Water wearies too, you know.

Why not forget we came here to get a good look

Too much light you must have said where fog frosts the window and the violets can't do another day. Caricature in the threshold moonlighting he wants to be a good moonlighter up and at 'em. This is hardly a recipe for the dripping sink keeps parachuting where are the parachutes. I must have walked too quickly by, make the eaves retain the water, lilacs flushed with a carrying hand look at that grip. Forget everything is the modest motto. I dug a deep hole. I put my leg in, my hand, the whole hokey pokey got blasphemous suddenly. Oh but someone else's hand is freezing, glove stuck to ice, particle board in the dump at the edge of town. I look like a good piece of limb in the redwood's limbs. Saw the twig crack, snap.

Why not look it up when you don't know what it means

Climbed the car alarm till the trees went dead. Here, the pancakes are still warm have another bite. I open the sockets, fresh fuzz into love letters whose are they I don't even know anyone called that. It's a shame about the interior limestone willing the day away from itself. Bright the undertaker with his shovel, the rearranged dirt. This is dailyness. No, it's a crane holding a fish lengthwise, a map. There's magenta stuck to my head you're not even looking. Crossed the mosquito bite once once once for permanence. Stilted drunk party slurring the cattails. But I don't wanna go. I will put on my clown suit, thickening behooves you somehow, your ankles pricked with what the wind. I will dance, slit the backs of my wrists.

Why not examine how time does not change much at all

Again June cupboards seeping heat. Park & ride summertime didn't you hear me through the floor last night I thought it was a romantic dehydration fit. Your life no story but the worm eating it. I can't hear over the flooded state park and bloated fish. Up higher go the clouds upon capped heads in maroon. The ingredients are all there. In June begging nestles under a bench and does not sing you to sleep. Penicillin which sticks the immune system with an eventual breakdown. Human hands upon the sparrow equals kicked from the nest. The carnival ride broke in half that's the second chipped plate in a row. Repeat after me: I will wash the pesticides off I will love strangers who look at me with more desire than you.

Love poem (tree minus limb and counting)

Here I am   enough
ochre petals   to talk
ringing another sigh
let   the flowers
be flowers   again
so exact   not hearing
the taste   envisioned
(fruit no   more
peaches) loose in
mouth   I this   this
for sweetly

Free my   I suppose
careful atop   sugar
branches   more
sought   one less
breaks   let's
song   my windy
in place   please
wider   grows salt
or these   hands
open   no opened
I   speed   sparkle

I woke

I woke, sticky vowels in my bed,
last century's songs whispering in my hands
like abandoned hotels. Each dollar crisp with rust,
how we'd prefer the avalanche on each other's heads
in the desert hospital. Look, I run very fast circles.
Clockwise. Counterclockwise. Modern shoes,
spaceships coated with sugar, the holiest war
I've ever frequented on the longest day of the year.
But did you remember to bring your sadness. I added
raisins to the bread, yeast thick in my hair, halved pomegranate sky.
The everything took the shape of a swift comb. I interpreted
it myself. Much the same moon repeating itself,
I forgot the rocks to beat my clothes against.
But I'm not one to talk, morning light overpowering sweat.
A sharp knife and/or a jagged can whips and the pain differs.
Could you call up the memory on the phone.
Could the snow be any louder.

Finding way (an apple or the thunk)

I

Exchanges the bathtub for swift cello
                              a clean break and all the odds stacked
          up calling my name   (the rafters)

Or, Your majesty the color is dim I am trying my heat on
                    for size.   Quick my speckled hen!   (out in the corner)
This painting bores or bleaches

                              the metaphor sleeps   (it is a nice nice bed)
          among me gripping your hair.

                    Sun short stops your freckles in mid–
speech   let's get quick   super daisy   (in the park)

      Where to get to?   All the cameras go click and nonetheless
                              I look at green and it doesn't.

Who's to know what consequences are neatly gifted
                              and without nametags?
                    Now we kick and cry   I suppose.   Enter
          and hear the latch snap (not my house but still a house)

Shed the sheep   place your foot on the piano pedal
                                        I am too away
                                        (an unpaved road)

Fire station   all alarms blaring —
                Have I grasped (the bell) tight enough for this exchange?
        Rescues the shouts
              in tiny market   (fresh fruit) engulfed.
                      All the children go scream.

And,   today is sheer (cloud) in my yard,
              hardly have I opened (my mouth) to let you —

      Figure the new (flowers)   the familiar sidestepped brown (grass)
            keeping   the overhead (jet) in view —

      What sound are you looking?

Because   inside the (dance hall) milling wouldn't let up
              dance crazy tango   on the (outskirts).
                However the breakdown happened
it is this much   (my hands).

Sound (the object)   a great dissonance dissolves (the bridge).

      The rough (substance)   I without you —

Bring the outside inside   play a mute (game)

       (the piano) and the piano   is a city never visited

      large (tower) looming

          (hat) floating downstream —

Through my chest, where were you

When you hand me the sparrow
                astonishment across my eyes like (happy birthday! A surprise
                        should stretch the lusty part of night)
I give the headache (head rush) a stern talking to —
                This is before some bombing, after thickness ran through my chest
                    (Where were you the night
                        what grievance took hold of stray dogs)

You keep marching. You keep the bed warm.
                The lovers sleep in meticulous forests.
                        Will you count to ten before —
            (We want to stage a good time, but not down your throat)

I am talking to myself (in sparrow) again.
                Quick quick the clock balks. Recognizing my love a stitched task.
                  I have much to tell you before the opening sky
                      leaves my shoelaces swollen —
            (This is the friendly part, we slip our hands up your back)

I yearn to fix the crooked part,
                hammer, screwdriver, jackhammer, sledgehammer
                    my side of split cotton —
            (O raveled sheets)   (Leave it to morning)

I go winged. Feathers stuck to coat.

I am inside this flag

Across stained taxi cab seats
the window broken in wrong places
so the rain.   With a dress like that
leave it up to the eyes.   Stuck in the door
a little silver a little language so I can
feel the weight of each drop on my umbrella.
            Come here my heart etched in tree trunks,
the wind catalyzing undoing, apples served
as sauce.   To explain the light
away I hold a handkerchief of the softest
silk blend.   Can I retexture the smile not meant
for me, will the museum lock its doors promptly
even though I am inside.   This flag I know burns
to the bone.   Suppose my one day off contains
shiny hinges and can fold at free will. Crack
of the fortune cookie   last call ringing through the bar —
            I love the actual
story, once you wipe your makeup off. How much
I want to touch your cheek, from across
the room, does not matter;   the contents of the doggy bag
making the dog sick.   Goodbye hail storm, goodbye
thick stalks of flowers.   When I sail the boat I end
halfway through the musical, the snappiest number,
    meet me here.

Rosary

Twilight thicket, ye arms are a badass melody
marking this quicksilver pleasure, wrapped in
the waves of a sea. I think it screams. But
sultry, to be honest. Not another blink of
the eye. Prehistoric matter in its posh place
up the hill yonder. I confuse with the best
of them my horse's mane, my man coming
home with a golden briefcase.

*

Yesterday stolen postcards erupted from
the chimney and I boxed the ashes. My
insides are wicked with war but
the kites keep the sky up. Flame in the lateral
position, back of my sweaty knee, won't you
please cancel the subscriptions.
My trip of the fat land is successful thus far.
Blood scurries the veins. Stays put.

*

There is a small fortune in my mouth some
of the time, laughing. The words popped out
I wasn't thinking so metaphorically speaking.
That 'ole toothy badger. That grass skirt so fit
for a stage of flowers. Truly a great mystery
getting all the more mysterious, I could be
the assembly line dust coating my luscious locks.
But not so dramatic. Truth: the sea's limited

movement, each swirl and heave in the back
and forth, never self-conscious never sick of itself.

*

Leaves falling and afterwards one could imagine
the tree a little sad. I pull out some glue, fuse my
indifference with my indifference. They fit nicely
together, stored in a hatbox, the land thick with
graves on a hill so snowy the graves are disappearing.
I look in a mirror. Overly in love we decide not
to speak. Call me squawker. I have mulch
and a matching cage.

*

I ready for departure, frost at the peephole,
hum at the tongue. The food is what you
would call homemade. Can't you smell the
plastic table decorated just so? I use the silver-
ware to hold my hair in place. My master doth
keep the wind pocketed, the sharp sun cold.
I go by taxi by train by plane by sex in a dirty
bathroom. Sorry, I forgot your name,
the bench is cold today.

*

Digging the backyard birds up, bones small as
sugar, grains scattering the ground. A seize of
melancholy last time the plains flooded, my
belongings caught in the current. But I was
a lust machine back in my Scorpio days.
Now I'm a Gemini and sit quietly with my

slippered feet on the rug. It's the wooded life.
There — the town drunk is ripping his shirt.
There — the postman dons new galoshes
and so on and so.

✶

And the lilacs across the pool table come into view,
a decision to water the indifference so it grows
at a steady pace. A most Hare Krishna day to you.
I was lounging til time did bring me back.
All the pleasantries erupted from your face and your
feet couldn't keep the sidewalk parallel. Like
a dusty bedside book. Like the atom particle
you saw minus magnifying glass.

✶

When I arrive the song asks to be let out.
Fortunate beloved with crusty lip caught
in the milk bottle. Just the other day I gave
in good, divided the pieces of sunset into
a little fairy tale. You look nice wearing the
moon in your hair, sparkle sparkle shine, I
want to let go. Sometimes I weave
for the fun. Sometimes I hum and
then I don't.

III

The waiting

A day going nest to falling
further dying and a bluster

meaning lost clocks and you.
Eye of tailpipes and unrung bells

like I jumped headfirst out of
the scented lovelessness.

Fatter chickens grow crates
for winter and atoms marry

in ash. Take my x my particleboard
history shoving the rain aside.

Cotton coffin with hands like yours.
Some malpractice going worse

flagged with thistled threads.
At your service

the moon breaks glass and glows.
Sketched mouth in the uprising.

*

Difference out of thimbled words
the artifacts. History's paged

thumbprints the cobbled platoon
breathing in unison. My self in

unison after memory in the spitting
stars. Time leaving the body

proofless utterly charged and whispers
this is your right foot this your left.

Scent of you all to myself the wind the
flawed bit of meat a crate for the bird.

*

Even kingdom come inside
your jowls from time to time

remaining. My brain shadow pinned
one farther day to snow. Light

and burdened the instance swirling
red the hummed streak beneath rock.

Illicit x in treetops singing night over.
You meet gainfully the docked

loneliness in splintered house
wept through I imagine.

*

Packaged land in forming reveals
a wish my sun I know no

lightfoot breeze. It is season-border
time but when the pilot light goes

ill and wavers. You gave the century
in a wink my gesture towards

the rest of living. Remainder of lips
in a dance then flew. I wore my hand

proud and personal waved and
sickened mirrors became

all wars the same an owl with
breaking eyes closed.

✳

Lamentations center cracked
wistful for light. The dead

not entirely. A tunnel containing
you till ways calendar

an arrangement of lush
theories circa magnetic field.

I wish my fear was smell to go by.
Easier in burnt mineral held

seal-tight some proof. I meet
the heart's transcription

in cared for cities gone.
Pain for star measured feet

continue which bloom under
first snow will streamline.

*

Like I was mimicking the gun
held thought-high the cobwebs

gathering corners. That threads
remain attached and jumping fall.

Paste the moment-moon to me.
No farther scent than now will

give you riper once upon a
battle and once upon

exchange. Swallowed leaves
to hold you down that

inside my chest you
might flow freely.

✳

Wait wanly lightfoot coffin
the x the stride bowed down to

bloom and full withdrawal. Lapsing
recognition the crates capsized

blown open. Years ago I sat
the middle swirl in salty rain.

A myth piecemealed like part of you
unknown to you a lake shimmering

in snow spread past the edges I
will not grasp the eyes.

*

Wired bullet to the dream
in vivid windowpane the

chipped paint that one may
graze and sucked stomach

to sky through door you
come carrying platter of century

extended heel to toe and closer
arms to take the creaking

medium hue and hand racket
which love me back.

*

Steadfast to meet a cloud cover
room in house in city

where the idea of you
poses light on shadow. No

valediction to tie the arms
no thread. Above what is cast

to air and drizzled chest sped up.
A pig in line and slips

where outside the snow I could
bear to clutch the world the intestines

running real through my fingers
my yes to you my knowing

trembled past the certainty
these tiny tufts of shame.

*

Death march in trumpet
blares. That cemeteries

garner the imposed giving back
brisk air to magnetic

move you. The earth
doubles back a moldy post a scent

of song where into hope
I may wager haze. Clean

nightfall. The horizon opens x
and ashes shine like lakes

at end of rope I hang
and hung you loving well.

*

A door shut where streets
creak. I take the barn for

letting loose the breathing
and structure stands.

My palm opening to feed the
reconstructed war some

scuffling pearls to pigs. I built
a house inside your shadow.

To whisper walnut and skin while
sleeping you remain too far.

Dead in mouth the chest
swallows and swallows.

*

A crate across the way
to which a timeline attests

to bones decayed the earth.
Fiery rain accumulates and stripped

clean plummets like money. You
step out of the way the x

calls out your name here the mud
and holding me back. I think

to see history's nails through
skin. I love(d) you like a wishing

well damp with sweat. The memory
cannot serve the fits and flights.

*

Inside the fabric bit by
shame a homecoming banner.

Bus stop outside the barn
my x and secret knock in sleet

the beginning of the next
yourself. A lifted face the

bleeding goat my God
that sky might leave me

handless. I do not want this
here. I know sounds

of cascading remains
subtle shifts in bed.

*

Forgotten designated chalk
and stone to harbor weeds.

The outline sprinting like identical
snowflakes to see what song

might appear in blades.
I drop you in distance the wheel

clatter the misshaped fire.
I came here to know the

dizzy lapped season the toiling
of your body alone returning

air sick and depleted this
lengthening which is also mine.

*

Target me to the owl the
echo in its framework.

Spoken of your melting marching
the plains my x in sky confinement.

Into a wagon I put the city grown
symmetrical weed cacophony.

Assimilate fear by pitch and
duration. I have a tent story a flower

for arrival waving I wave my
ribs like train and steam.

IV

Getting ready for time

Careless yellow   in the outcroppings
            like a million years   exaggerated turnpike—
        Fearless shoes strung telephone wire   heave-hoing it
every car ride to countryside   dressed in participle fashion—
        Jump up and out   for *I must be, or I could not*
empty myself for sleep   *in a strange room*   trickles the widest river
        down to   my God I must have loved
even a tattered kite   struggling the wind—

*

Outskirts a statue   covered with crow
        remains   *a wet seed wild in the hot blind earth*   tracking
verbs in translation   quitting themselves—
        My mouth seeds itself the same day   for abundant sleep
in a bed I long for my own   cave-like conditions—
        Where red is true red   doubts penny themselves
fountains my streamlined breath   in need of nothing
        but whatever I am—

*

Roll over, window   chain link fence   that bird
        is restless red feathers   *as though the clotting*
        which is you   *had dissolved*   *into the myriad original motion*
        a ball clopping goose down pavement—
When you get to   unfinished sentences
        will the scurry of mice bring you back further?
Testify testify   unto the she-ship   rolling
        waves lessen near shore   a quiver of a gift—

*

Back to back   no height,   identical syntax—
     An urn chipped by loving   ashes so many
further away than seeing shapes   *the dead earth. It lies dead*
       and warm upon me   the cocoon sea, splintering—
Knots in the pond   barnacle filament
      where I walk blue and sunny   in mustard seed
upon thee   my crackling
       lest the bridge splatter and sleep—

*

In another dream   hush please   static pillow
     clothes hang   slow and wet   *poised like a bloody egg*
upon a crest of thunderheads   wild with sulfur   fastened   pale—
     Bequeath the child-conceiving   streaked city street
where finger tips   halfway grope   the market's sunflowers—
     An egg falls   through the cracks
my chalky silhouette   leaps back in
     when I tire of staring—

*

Time change   a room with lovers uncovered
     dresser statue   dipped in dust
a motionless hand lifted   *above the profound desolation*   *of the ocean*—
     Temperature at the back   of my neck
works words   into coals beneath fire   the ash-slick floor
     damp park at dusk   condensation   out of fortitude—
A hum   slightly bandaging
     each slow murmur   in red and fizzled blue—

*

Reaching for   the gray-lipped pheasant   dutiful soldier
          tatters torn from the flat darkness strung skin   settling—
Each poppy   on ice   beneath fresh snow
          where I came here to weep clean   *and turned backside out*
a salty hand   film smacking against itself   dissolving—
O grip the marble   the lever a harness   this abandoned bus
          stop's fliers wing   through   the wind
                the sky has no use   cities upon cities upon towns—

*

Moths knit themselves to the light   your ocean
          is foaming at the mouth   hush hush   séance of spring
the holes filled with distance   *beyond the land*   I want to herald
          hurdle through   the bird the basket   chipped paint like wet stars—
Thicket song matches the berries   in forging—
          Under foot   snapped twigs   pickpocketing wind—
Let the moon-stumbling   walk keep my feet
          adrift   for the breeze   is picking up—

Hand clap

On stage to closer war cries
sun & paper lantern fuse
the early bluebells
meaning dream is not
so levelheaded that cheek upon cheek
wrestles me to you with atoms
winged the periscope hymns
scent my architecture open-
ended wire & balloon stem can't
you hear me shaking there are
muffins the knife splitting
them open is a stick figure.

Wing for unaware

Leafless unto me where working
between drone & shadow

how much flinging I have conjured
laid bare on pristine streets

similarities next to yellowed
the original circumference of the earth
a tighter chest to hem the ribs in place

I am walking through few reasons at a clip
when wishing sprints and this is not
the eagle soar that breeds turned
cheek admiring from afar

when I go back I do not want to
hold fast the dying at my feet &
double-minded spinning top
which glides on tile unaware of pull & slow

these tears spared under sheets
snowed pocket & hot rod

my tiny war a star in sky

*

Blistered history for today
also the head shot photography & lunch
@ 1 w/ friend for lettuce and blue insistence

my wrists ingesting more magnitude
hard & subtle line of spaceship rising

unwritten rhetoric of pulse a colorless dream
whiter whites & fruitless blacks

no greater pain than sharp sky above
a wound with eye to see & spits & closes

*

Consistent miracle within the egret's nest
the aging cypress the fetching of sticks
an arm urging movement to traffic stopped

I feel the heat myself & think no less
of weathered past caging the ground
o that loss precedes the alphabet & tangles here

a bit of ear for fertilizing the garden

a housedress to weep in sky

I confess my limbs are inaccurate
for steepness but low to the plains
the dogs run unhindered & eat where they may

Dialogue of sea

Bruised lamb I say
       (conceived in a pit)
how walk your legs
       (path around town)
I quiver I lackluster
speed sipping the lights
lest borrowing browns
       (till death do us part)
Darkly mirrored hand
       (sand in the bag)
upon oath   orator   orb
       (the heart is not shaped like one)

Nocturne 1

Unknown to closure the rabid alley
run through. Night & plum in plot.

A lengthened tremble over wine,
a pale percent of past to meet you

weak in tides trickling out. Damp
enough to drop your hand I fear

the sparse fields too soon for winter
& browning singular within you.

Perpetual middle. Makeshift house
swaying from roof in recluse. The cremated

sea bends with box & branch, finds its way
to drain. Most heads held high despite.

Enough liminal love wound through
cardboard faces reaches song.

Young & crammed lie the dying in bed.
From the moon I can bear to hear

each way you turn away in wooden chair
a watery escape to me you pulse, you platitude.

Nocturne 2

Benched craze of the wool heart,
pulse in the leg reminiscent, rescued.

My urgent miscellaneous *to do* is
the kite sweeping our heads is the

waiting shoulder. How long has the lake
shimmered in touch, finds itself missing

while I cover my territory, returning
the gifts one by one, flowers on tightrope

in place. Again for you I wait, a
fault line. Stepping into the emergency

like lightning-struck child, the list so long
our bodies cannot stretch & make do.

I can only catch an honest eye temporarily,
the sand lapping rocks which you name.

The blue photograph I trace to the sun
& the mist you wear worn only by me

is a lingering held breath
the fragrance of fear which is home.

Nocturne 3

Fingering the edges conventionally,
a marriage, a sweet-toothed swan

skimming its way through pond & pinnacle.
A fate, the hands clasping, retired bullock

in bed of hay retrieving glassy sheen.
October free fall. Bits of wind near seizure.

Can happen inside the circumference of loyalty,
a bashful heat from bodies, breach, lurch, search

me till raw limbs. You, farm-like among
apple trees, wed to your self a whelping

wing, mistake & Pythagorean theorem.
A plow soft with rust curdles hardening earth.

Please tell me how to exit rooms unnoticed but
with a kiss o exhaled wire & seeing through.

In the manner of dying

I

I came nohow whoosh whoosh
to the field not recognizing me.
Along the protractor merges the poem
with what it does not want to say.
I tried to be a good tree, covering
the ground with blossoms,
cherry pits choking the birds.
Taxicab must in the skyline else
forgive church bells in breaking.
What else do you want me to say?
I set the loyalty on fire but my skin
still burns. My scarf isn't so warm.
On the corner the sparrow sells itself
and the rest is a newsletter unread
on fat country porches.
Not to drift further, resources,
comes the dream of dead Nathan
only half dead, calling his mistakes
out through a megaphone.
When I die I will probably stay dead.
If I hurry the words my mouth will clamp.
My bit soaked with what I couldn't.

II

In the natural history museum
mummies married to glass.
My breath was unbecoming,
rocks resembling backyards.
A hefty woman slings a slim
girl over her shoulders.
And the poem hurries.
I'm sorry, I say, I didn't mean
to step on you.
That's OK says the little girl,
that's OK.

III

Fine the land stretched over
my stomach. Please and thank you.
The pond guarantees to mask
the dirt underneath.
My illness wasn't as ill as my other illness.
But the pine trees look carnivorous
because I am a great misinterpreter.
Sea floor swing dances a riot.
Hoot hoot, the owl plummets.

IV

The crucifix took the shape of a broken kite.
I stood tall at softball and missed.
The poem confused its love with a twitch.
Too many fantastic party drinks,
I drag myself home by a wilted scarf.
Wake up, I say, the hierarchy
is sandwiched to substitute for dinner.
But I'm not hungry, comes the reply,
maybe later—

Peephole

I go away for awhile.
The chickens capture
kernels and shake
a bit. Cool sun
on sand, ice peopling
itself under. Planned
to restaurant but cabinet
looks good. I like wood
digesting in termites,
stuffed the mouth
is slow. Could be
calloused hands.

I go away awhile.
It wasn't that tempting.
An animal shedding
machine. Icelandic tree
gripping through
winter. Sometimes
I put myself in the
rooming house where
I clutch rain. Wilted
llama hair in the
socks, the frenzy I
break my neck open for.

THE IOWA POETRY PRIZE &
EDWIN FORD PIPER POETRY AWARD WINNERS

1987

Elton Glaser, *Tropical Depressions*

Michael Pettit, *Cardinal Points*

1988

Bill Knott, *Outremer*

Mary Ruefle, *The Adamant*

1989

Conrad Hilberry, *Sorting the Smoke*

Terese Svoboda, *Laughing Africa*

1990

Philip Dacey, *Night Shift at the Crucifix Factory*

Lynda Hull, *Star Ledger*

1991

Greg Pape, *Sunflower Facing the Sun*

Walter Pavlich, *Running near the End of the World*

1992

Lola Haskins, *Hunger*

Katherine Soniat, *A Shared Life*

1993

Tom Andrews, *The Hemophiliac's Motorcycle*

Michael Heffernan, *Love's Answer*

John Wood, *In Primary Light*

1994

James McKean, *Tree of Heaven*

Bin Ramke, *Massacre of the Innocents*

Ed Roberson, *Voices Cast Out to Talk Us In*

1995

Ralph Burns, *Swamp Candles*

Maureen Seaton, *Furious Cooking*

1996
  Pamela Alexander, *Inland*
  Gary Gildner, *The Bunker in the Parsley Fields*
  John Wood, *The Gates of the Elect Kingdom*
1997
  Brendan Galvin, *Hotel Malabar*
  Leslie Ullman, *Slow Work through Sand*
1998
  Kathleen Peirce, *The Oval Hour*
  Bin Ramke, *Wake*
  Cole Swensen, *Try*
1999
  Larissa Szporluk, *Isolato*
  Liz Waldner, *A Point Is That Which Has No Part*
2000
  Mary Leader, *The Penultimate Suitor*
2001
  Joanna Goodman, *Trace of One*
  Karen Volkman, *Spar*
2002
  Lesle Lewis, *Small Boat*
  Peter Jay Shippy, *Thieves' Latin*
2003
  Michele Glazer, *Aggregate of Disturbances*
  Dainis Hazners, *(some of) The Adventures of Carlyle, My Imaginary Friend*
2004
  Megan Johnson, *The Waiting*
  Susan Wheeler, *Ledger*